Tackle Box Troubles

Fish Tale #2: Bucky Bucktail & Tommy Topwater

SUSAN DUKE
Illustrated by Jose Tecson

Also by Susan Duke:
Tackle Box Troubles Fish Tale #1: Sammy Spinner

To order additional copies of this book, contact:
Xlibris
844-714-8691
www.Xlibris.com
Orders@Xlibris.com

ISBN: Softcover   978-1-6698-7777-6
       Hardcover   978-1-6698-7779-0
       EBook   978-1-6698-7778-3

Print information available on the last page

Rev. date: 05/25/2023

Thank you to my husband, parents, brothers, sisters-in-law, and friends for the support you've given me throughout this journey!

Thank you, also to my editor, Rosemary Baker, for the guidance, suggestions, and effort you've provided to make this a wonderful story.

For fishermen who spend hours casting and reeling:
Remember that it's fishing not catching!
There will be days when not much goes right.
Other days, lots of fish will be caught,
And your smile will be bright!

For my niece, Olivia, and nephews, Duke, Hawke, and Killian:
While spending time on the lake waiting for your bait to hook into another fish, turn off your phones and use your eyes and ears to experience the beautiful show nature offers you.

For the families who have spent time with me in the Northwoods:
Thank you for years of amazing experiences and wonderful memories made during our vacations together in Northern Wisconsin. I'll always smile when remembering the moments we spent together playing on the water, sitting around large campfires, catching big fish, looking up at the stars, enjoying everything outdoors, and laughing for hours as we told stories in our cabins.

1

With the motor rumbling, the S.S. Betsy rocked back and forth in the rippling lake water. The red boat, safely tied to a wooden pier, eagerly waited to take the tackle box full of lures to a very secret fishing spot.

Each lure inside the tackle box could barely wait for its next fishing adventure. A partly sunny sky and a slight breeze in the air made it the ideal time to dive into the chilly water to catch big fish.

While they waited to go fishing, the lures listened to the lakeside sounds of the Northwoods that filled the air around the boat.

A young fox ran back and forth along the shoreline as its teeth crunched through snail shells. A woodpecker rhythmically drummed its beak into the bark of a tall tree. A family of ducks paddled through the water near floating driftwood that bounced along the rocky shore.

Before the boat pulled away from the pier, Bucky Bucktail decided it was a good time to review the fishing troubles from the season that had led to missed catches and frustrated fishermen.

The most common trouble was when lures got tangled up in patches of long, leafy seaweed along the shoreline. Other lures sank too deep into dark water. Here their hooks became wedged between boulders at the bottom of the lake.

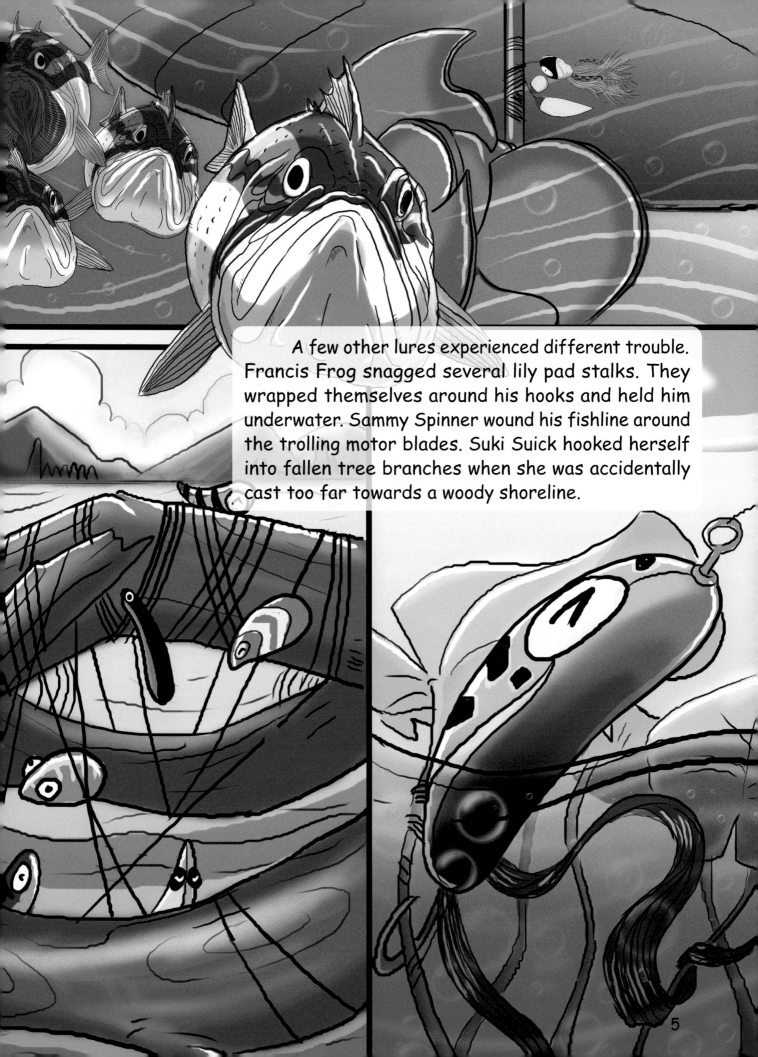

A few other lures experienced different trouble. Francis Frog snagged several lily pad stalks. They wrapped themselves around his hooks and held him underwater. Sammy Spinner wound his fishline around the trolling motor blades. Suki Suick hooked herself into fallen tree branches when she was accidentally cast too far towards a woody shoreline.

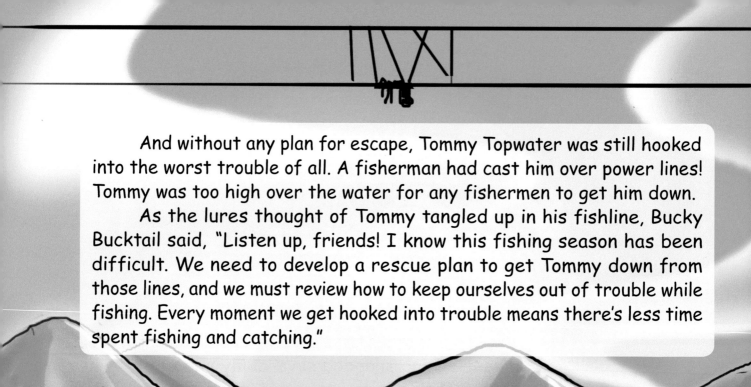

And without any plan for escape, Tommy Topwater was still hooked into the worst trouble of all. A fisherman had cast him over power lines! Tommy was too high over the water for any fishermen to get him down.

As the lures thought of Tommy tangled up in his fishline, Bucky Bucktail said, "Listen up, friends! I know this fishing season has been difficult. We need to develop a rescue plan to get Tommy down from those lines, and we must review how to keep ourselves out of trouble while fishing. Every moment we get hooked into trouble means there's less time spent fishing and catching."

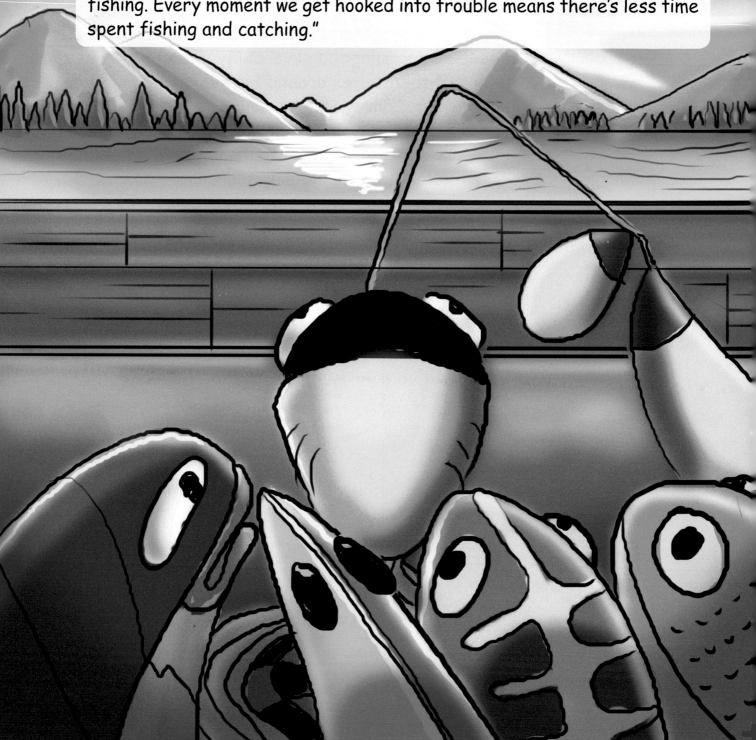

Sammy Spinner replied, "Bucky, you taught me that catching big fish in the Northwoods is not easy. But you never told me that some lures don't make it back into the tackle box when they go fishing! I cannot believe Tommy Topwater is stuck hanging from those power lines. It's very dangerous out there! I'm beginning to think fishing is not the sport for me."

7

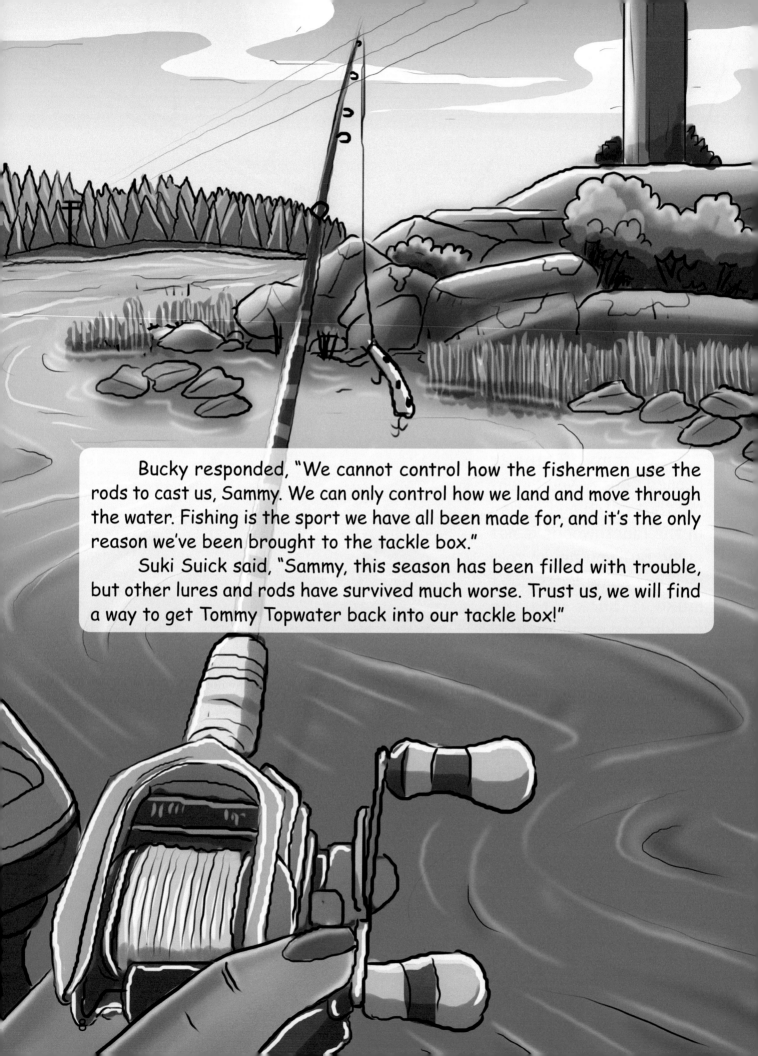

Bucky responded, "We cannot control how the fishermen use the rods to cast us, Sammy. We can only control how we land and move through the water. Fishing is the sport we have all been made for, and it's the only reason we've been brought to the tackle box."

Suki Suick said, "Sammy, this season has been filled with trouble, but other lures and rods have survived much worse. Trust us, we will find a way to get Tommy Topwater back into our tackle box!"

"And if we can't find a way to help Tommy down, at least we'll get to visit with him every time the boat floats under those power lines. When we look up, we'll see him hanging from the fishline tangled all around him. I suppose that's better than having him lost forever at the bottom of a cold lake," a short stickbait lure said sadly.

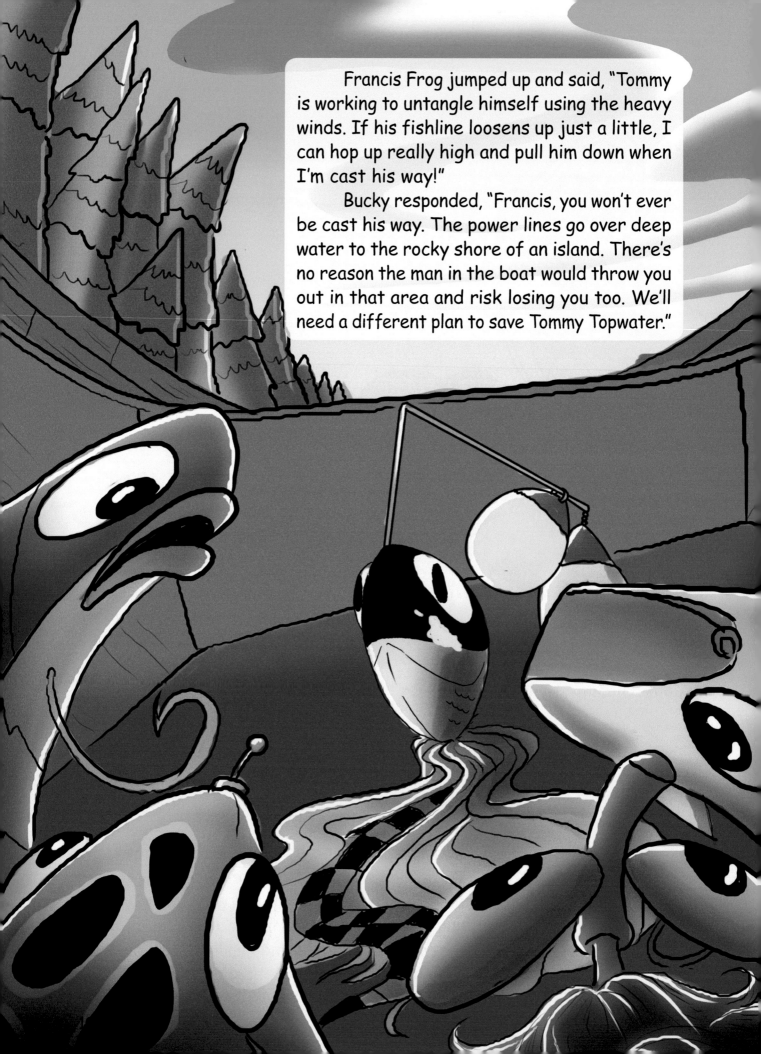

Francis Frog jumped up and said, "Tommy is working to untangle himself using the heavy winds. If his fishline loosens up just a little, I can hop up really high and pull him down when I'm cast his way!"

Bucky responded, "Francis, you won't ever be cast his way. The power lines go over deep water to the rocky shore of an island. There's no reason the man in the boat would throw you out in that area and risk losing you too. We'll need a different plan to save Tommy Topwater."

Francis responded, "Once upon a time, there was a bucktail lure attached to a fishing rod."

"What are you doing?" Bucky asked, sounding annoyed.

Francis answered, "I'm going to tell a story of fishing lure trouble and survival. It will show Sammy that Tommy can be rescued and safely returned to our tackle box. You know, so he won't quit fishing."

Bucky rolled his eyes and said, "I don't believe that a story is going to help Tommy or Sammy right now."

"It may not help, but it might be nice to hear as we wait to go fish. Go ahead Francis. Tell us the story," Sammy said.

Francis began again, "Once upon a time, Bucky Bucktail was attached to a fishing rod named Mr. Rodafeller. Bucky and Mr. Rodafeller worked very well together. They caught many long fish with lots of sharp teeth. That made the fishermen in this boat extremely happy."

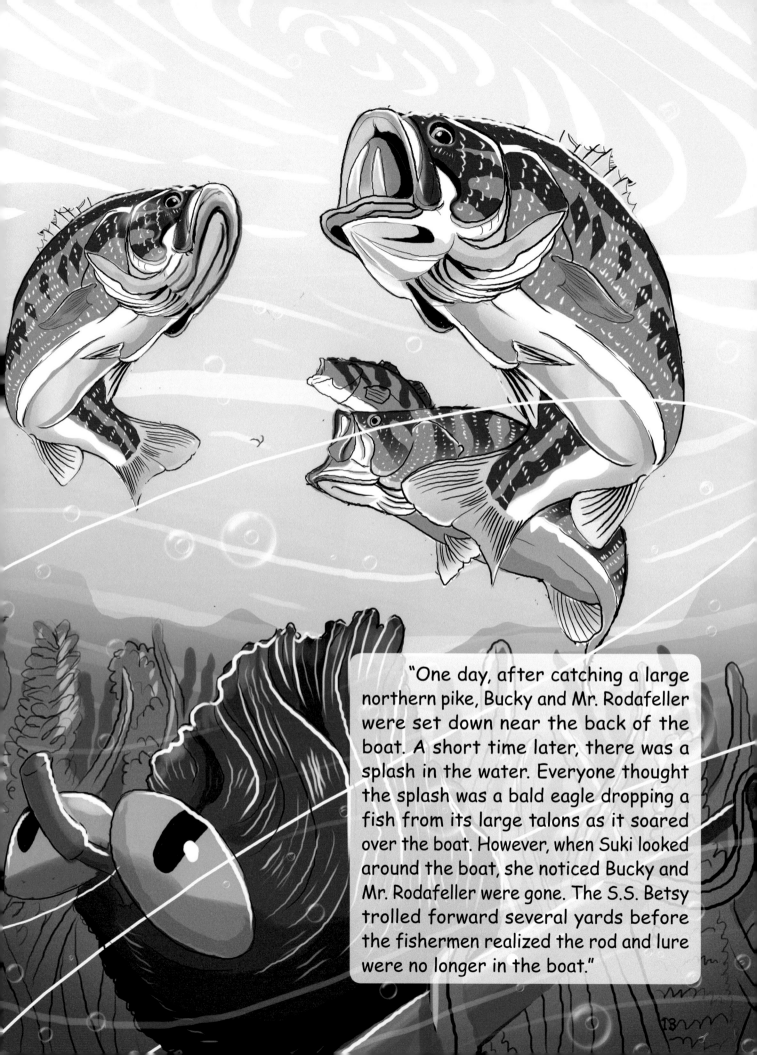

"One day, after catching a large northern pike, Bucky and Mr. Rodafeller were set down near the back of the boat. A short time later, there was a splash in the water. Everyone thought the splash was a bald eagle dropping a fish from its large talons as it soared over the boat. However, when Suki looked around the boat, she noticed Bucky and Mr. Rodafeller were gone. The S.S. Betsy trolled forward several yards before the fishermen realized the rod and lure were no longer in the boat."

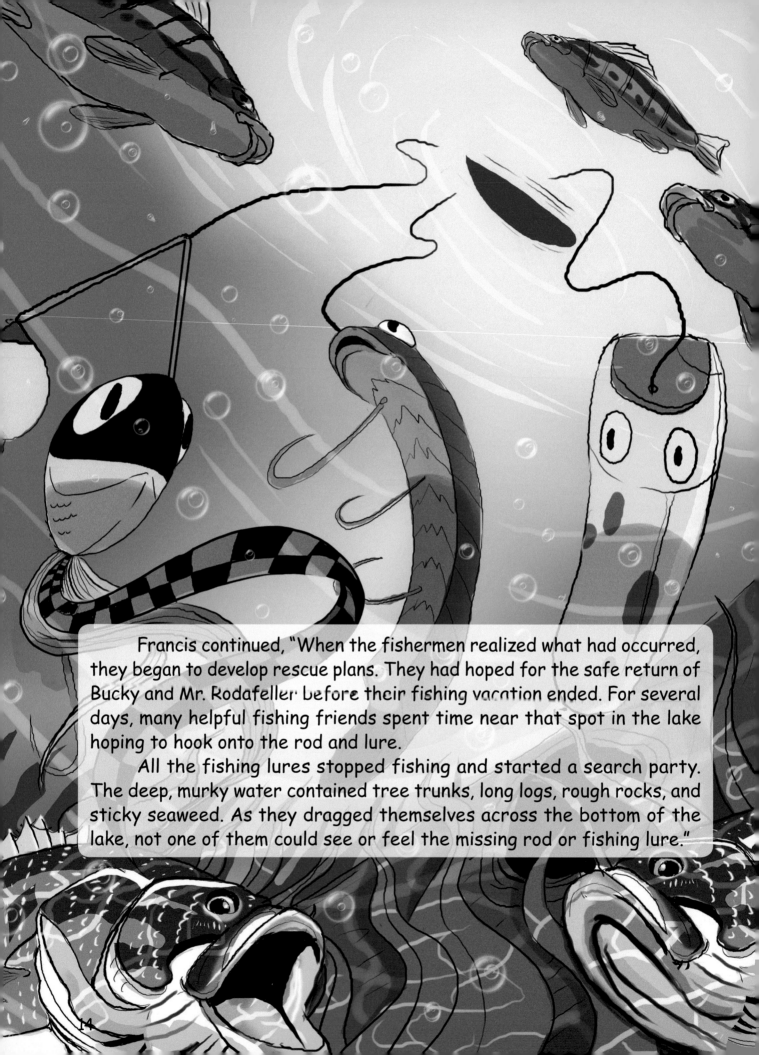

Francis continued, "When the fishermen realized what had occurred, they began to develop rescue plans. They had hoped for the safe return of Bucky and Mr. Rodafeller before their fishing vacation ended. For several days, many helpful fishing friends spent time near that spot in the lake hoping to hook onto the rod and lure.

All the fishing lures stopped fishing and started a search party. The deep, murky water contained tree trunks, long logs, rough rocks, and sticky seaweed. As they dragged themselves across the bottom of the lake, not one of them could see or feel the missing rod or fishing lure."

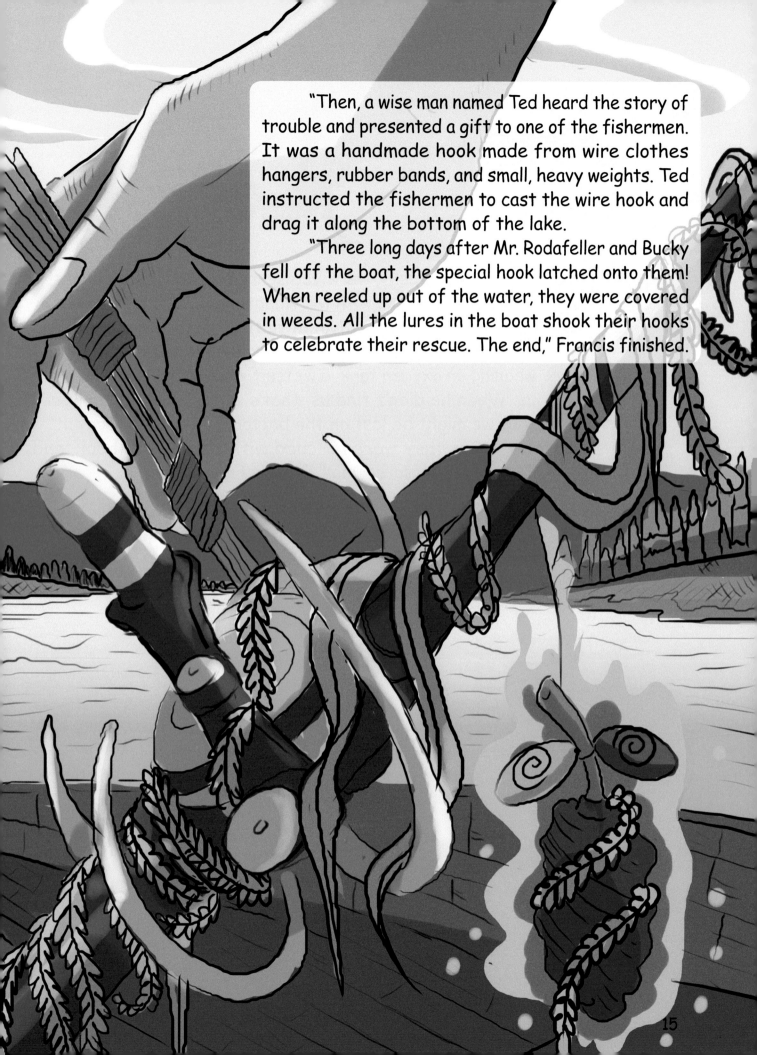

"Then, a wise man named Ted heard the story of trouble and presented a gift to one of the fishermen. It was a handmade hook made from wire clothes hangers, rubber bands, and small, heavy weights. Ted instructed the fishermen to cast the wire hook and drag it along the bottom of the lake.

"Three long days after Mr. Rodafeller and Bucky fell off the boat, the special hook latched onto them! When reeled up out of the water, they were covered in weeds. All the lures in the boat shook their hooks to celebrate their rescue. The end," Francis finished.

"Wow! Bucky, were you scared when you were on the bottom of the lake with Mr. Rodafeller?" Sammy asked.

Bucky answered, "Not at first. I knew the fishermen and lures were looking for us. I also saw Alex, the resort owner, wearing an oxygen tank, a wetsuit, and a mask searching for us. When he didn't find us, that's when I started to worry that we might be lost on the bottom of the lake forever."

"But they *were* rescued with the special hook, and Tommy can be saved too!" Francis Frog jumped in.

Suki Suick leaned over and said, "I remember a time when Bucky found himself in much worse trouble. Francis, do you remember when he hooked himself into Lucy?" she asked.

Francis Frog replied, "Oh, yes I do! Bucky wrapped himself up in such serious trouble that he needed surgery to be saved! Suki, you should share that story."

Sammy Spinner smiled and said, "It sounds to me like this is going to be a day filled with fishing stories all about Bucky."

"Lucky me," Bucky Bucktail replied sarcastically.

Before Suki started the story, Francis shouted out, "Hey, look down the pier! Here comes the fisherman with the long bamboo cane pole. Maybe he's developed a plan to rescue Tommy Topwater!"

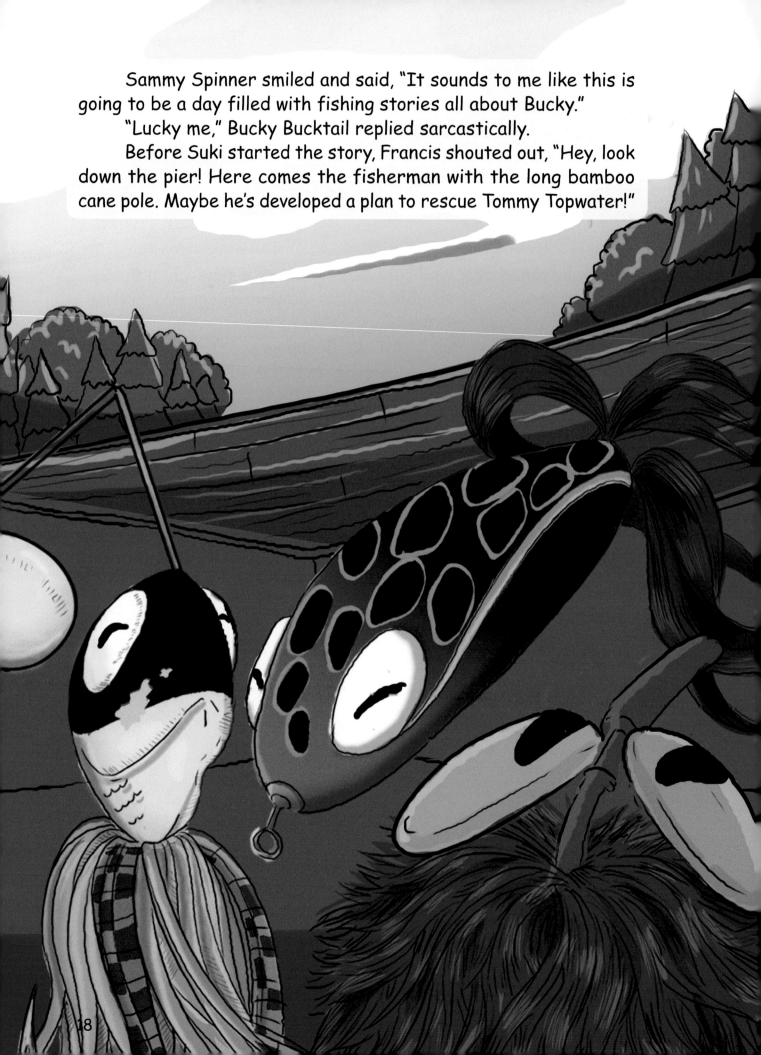

"He's also bringing the dog. Quick, cover up your hooks and close the tackle box!" Bucky Bucktail instructed with urgency in his voice.

The fisherman backed the S.S. Betsy away from the pier and sped off in the direction of where Tommy Topwater was tangled up in the power lines, high above the lake.

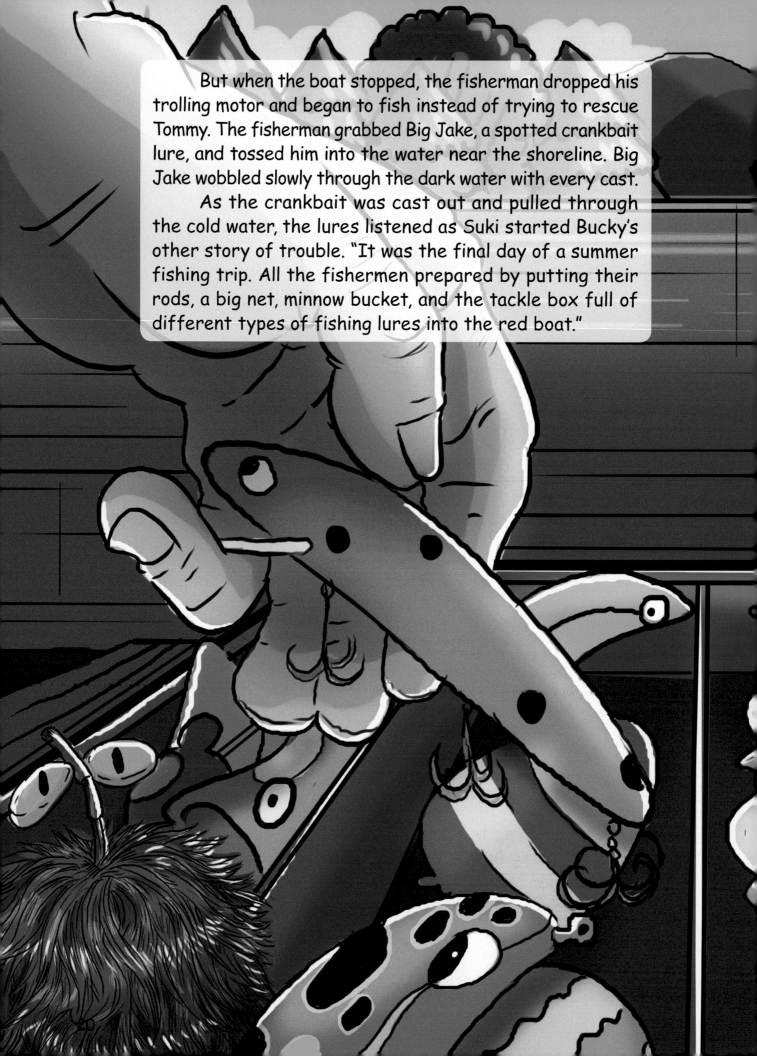

But when the boat stopped, the fisherman dropped his trolling motor and began to fish instead of trying to rescue Tommy. The fisherman grabbed Big Jake, a spotted crankbait lure, and tossed him into the water near the shoreline. Big Jake wobbled slowly through the dark water with every cast.

As the crankbait was cast out and pulled through the cold water, the lures listened as Suki started Bucky's other story of trouble. "It was the final day of a summer fishing trip. All the fishermen prepared by putting their rods, a big net, minnow bucket, and the tackle box full of different types of fishing lures into the red boat."

Suki continued, "While the fishermen prepared the fishing gear, their dogs, one of whom was named Lucy, swam in the water and ran along the shoreline."

Bucky Bucktail interrupted, "Most of the lures rested inside the tackle box, but some lures enjoyed the sunshine on the deck of the boat. That's what caused the problem. Some lures' hooks were not covered up. But we learned a lesson that day: Cover up your hooks! Now, can we please talk about a rescue plan for Tommy Topwater?"

Suki cheerfully said, "After this story." Then she continued, "All of a sudden, the dogs started to chase each other up and down the pier. Lucy jumped into the boat, out of the boat, back into the boat, and then out of the boat again. I don't speak dog, so I'm not sure what those dogs said to each other, but Lucy was barking and having fun."

Musky Ike leaned over to Sammy and said, "Obviously, one dog suggested that jumping in and out of the boat would be much more fun than swimming. The other dog agreed, and the great dog chase began."

22

Suki Suick continued the story, "Bucky Bucktail was just about to doze off when suddenly Lucy's leg grabbed one of Bucky's hooks as she jumped out of the boat. Bucky was violently tugged off the boat, and he flopped through the air as Lucy sprinted back and forth on the pier. When the yelping dog finally sat down, Bucky swung himself around and grabbed onto Lucy with two more hooks."

Bucky interrupted, "Yes, because I was terrified of being thrown into the lake and lost for days again! I needed to think of something fast. I thought more hooks in the leg was a good idea. Lucy did not like my hooks stuck in her leg, and she let the entire lake know it."

23

Suki went on with the story, "Lucy screamed so loudly that her long, wailing cries echoed around the lake. I worried Lucy was going to eat Bucky because she started snapping at him with her huge teeth. But the fisherman came to the rescue just in time! He flung his body on top of Lucy and protected Bucky from her long teeth."

Francis Frog jumped in and hollered out, "That's when the surgery began! The fisherman cut Bucky's hooks off to free him from Lucy. Bucky's scream scared four loons and several other birds off the water!"

"Of course I screamed, Francis! Do you have any idea how painful that moment of trouble was for me?" Bucky asked.

As a large bald eagle flew over the boat, Musky Ike finished the story. "In the end, Bucky was tossed around and lost some hooks. However, he was saved from the dog, his big hooks were replaced, and he still catches huge fish every season. He hasn't quit fishing and neither should you, Sammy Spinner."

"That moment of trouble is also why Bucky smells so awful when he comes back into our tackle box. After that day, Bucky never shakes the weeds loose or dries his fur when he comes in from fishing," Suki Suick shared.

Bucky said, "That's because I don't want to get hooked into a dog or fall off the boat and be lost for days in the water again. So, yes, I get into the tackle box as soon as I get back onto the boat."

"Now, before the boat moves to another fishing spot, can we please focus on the rescue plan to help untangle Tommy from the power lines?" Bucky asked.

Francis Frog leaned over to Sammy and quietly whispered, "Bucky was feeling a bit upset and very jealous because Lucy was spoiled with attention, love, and dog treats after the trouble was over.

"Unfortunately, Bucky was punished. He was left on the pier with his cut-off hooks, while the rest of us went out fishing."

Bucky said, "I was not jealous of a dog. I was upset about missing the final summer day of fishing. Remember, that's our goal, to catch big fish! Also, I was not being punished! My hooks were in pieces, and I was unable to do my job. That's the reason the fishermen left me behind on the pier. Fishing lures don't get punished."

Sammy smiled and said, "Bucky, I think you were very brave. Getting hooked into a dog sounds like serious trouble."

Bucky replied, "Thanks, Sammy. We all learned from that trouble. Now the fishermen keep us in the tackle box or keep our hooks covered when we aren't being cast out into the water."

"Yep, after Bucky's trouble, I always try to keep my hooks covered when I'm not fishing," Francis Frog croaked.

As the lures finished their stories, the fisherman in the red boat used his fishing rod to form a figure eight in the water. Suddenly, there was a strike on the fishline. The tip of the fishing rod was pulled down and curved towards the water.

Bucky, Suki, and Sammy watched the exciting action. They knew Big Jake was using his powerful personality and huge hooks to catch this big fish. "Fish on! Fish on!" Musky Ike and Francis Frog yelled.

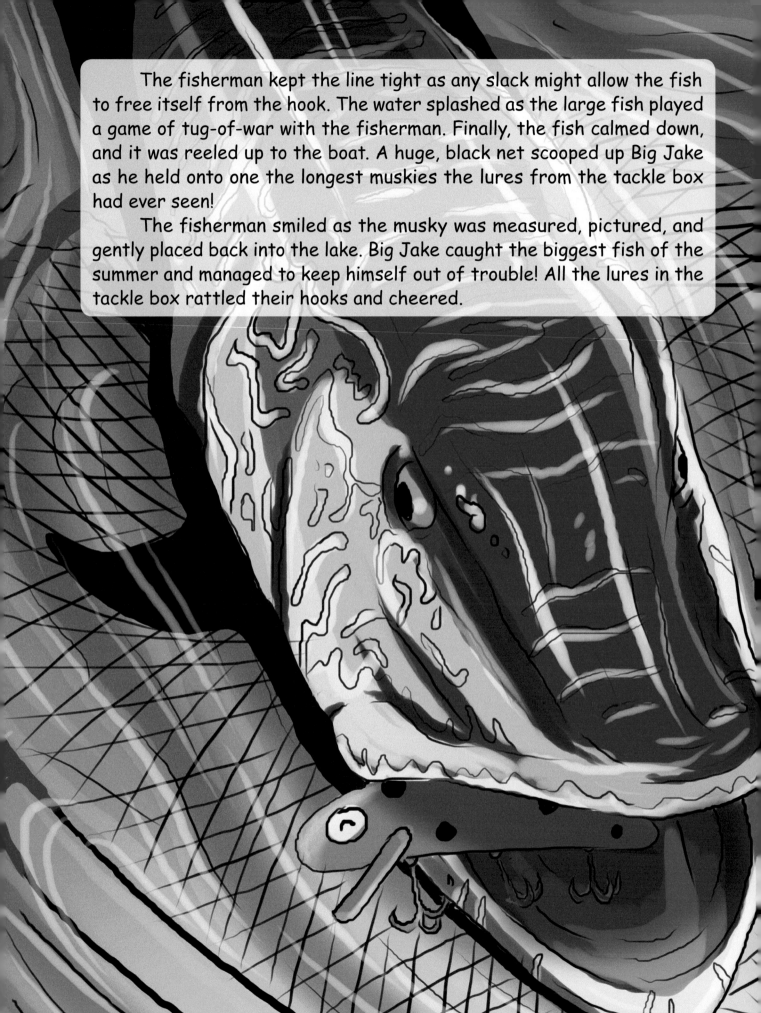

The fisherman kept the line tight as any slack might allow the fish to free itself from the hook. The water splashed as the large fish played a game of tug-of-war with the fisherman. Finally, the fish calmed down, and it was reeled up to the boat. A huge, black net scooped up Big Jake as he held onto one the longest muskies the lures from the tackle box had ever seen!

The fisherman smiled as the musky was measured, pictured, and gently placed back into the lake. Big Jake caught the biggest fish of the summer and managed to keep himself out of trouble! All the lures in the tackle box rattled their hooks and cheered.

High up on the power lines, Tommy Topwater had a perfect bird's-eye view of Jake's musky catch and release. And Tommy realized that he truly enjoyed watching the action from high above the water.

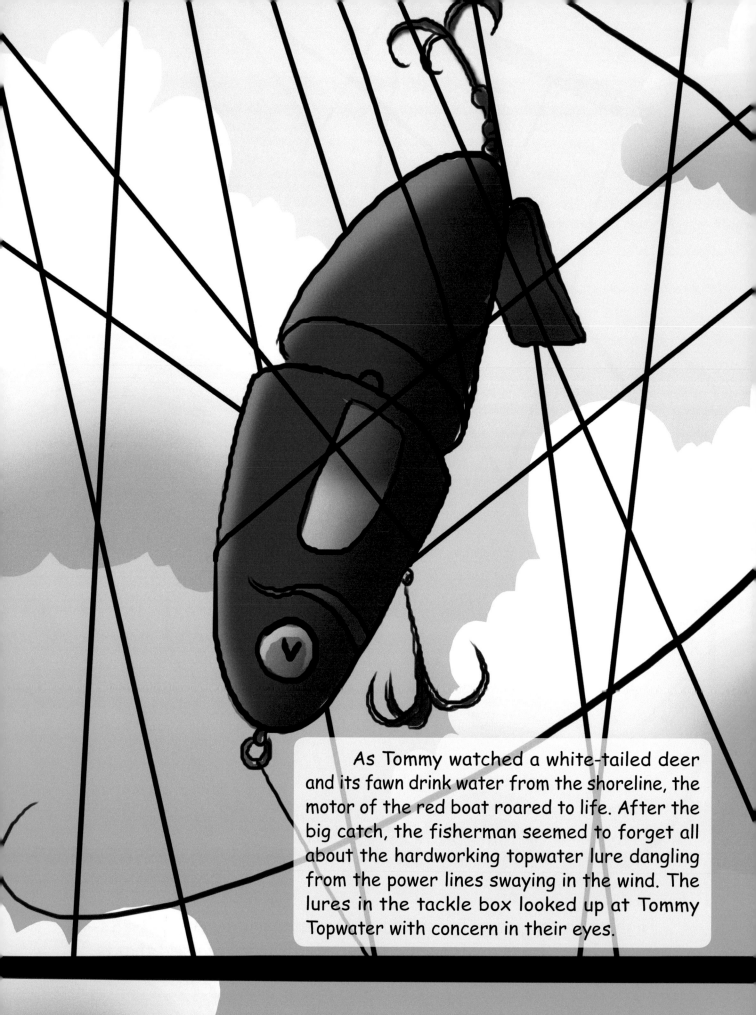

As Tommy watched a white-tailed deer and its fawn drink water from the shoreline, the motor of the red boat roared to life. After the big catch, the fisherman seemed to forget all about the hardworking topwater lure dangling from the power lines swaying in the wind. The lures in the tackle box looked up at Tommy Topwater with concern in their eyes.

Bucky Bucktail shouted, "We'll be back, Tommy. I promise! We'll develop a plan to free you from those power lines!"

Tommy looked down at the lures in Tackle Box Troubles and yelled, "Don't worry about me for now! I've enjoyed watching lots of fish get caught. Also, at sunset the water along the shoreline seems to turn the color of a golden penny. It is so beautiful! I wonder what the view will be like from up here in the winter."

As the sunshine hid behind a tall cedar tree, Suki Suick said, "You see, Sammy, sometimes when a lure gets into trouble, it turns out to be a wonderful experience."

Bucky added, "I believe being tangled up and hanging high from the power lines is better than being hooked into a dog's leg."

"That may be true," Musky Ike said, "but Tommy hasn't felt a frigid winter night in the Northwoods. I'm sure he'll be seeking our help when we return next summer to catch big fish."

"Or maybe," Francis Frog jumped in with a hopeful voice, "just maybe, a bunch of those small ice-fishing lures and their rods will be able to pull him down this winter!"

"Oh, Francis. You need to learn more about ice fishing. That's never going to happen. Those lures fish with short rods," Bucky said.

Tackle Box TROUBLES

As the fisherman returned to the pier and secured his boat, Musky Ike said, "I have an idea. We should ask other lures that have been tangled up and rescued for their ideas about how we can help Tommy Topwater."

Sammy Spinner responded, "That's a great idea! We will listen to their stories and learn how those lures were rescued. Then we can develop a perfect plan to retrieve Tommy from the power lines. Which fishing lures have a good story of trouble and survival to share?"

Francis Frog hopped up and shouted, "I think we should share Brittney Beaver's story of her tangled-up trouble in the shallow river!"

Musky Ike said, "We also learned a lot from Walter Walker's tangled-up trouble with a shoe, or was it a foot?"

Suki Suick said, "Oh, my favorite is when David Dardevle, with his silly sense of humor, got tangled up in trouble with...."

Bucky Bucktail interrupted, "I'm worried we're getting hooked in the trouble of distraction. We don't have time to get tangled up in storytelling. Let's start developing a plan to rescue Tommy Topwater before snowflakes start to fall and a freezing Northwoods winter arrives!"

A fishing lure from the bottom of the tackle box replied, "I have a perfect plan when you're ready to listen."

Characters from the Tackle Box

Suki Suick: A green-and-black striped, orange-bottomed, wooden jerk bait with pink lips. She has three large hooks and an adjustable, metal tail. Suki rips through thick weeds while catching musky, northern pike, and other long fish.

Bucky Bucktail: A two-bladed, in-line bucktail bait with a metal body covered in black, synthetic fur that hides his treble hooks. His orange and green blades spin as he is pulled through dark water catching long northern pike and musky.

Sammy Spinner: A scissors-style spinnerbait with a multicolored skirt covering his hook. He has two yellow and red blades that spin above his body as he is pulled through the water, fishing for bass, walleye, northern pike, and musky.

Francis Frog: A green, dark-spotted, rubber frog with weedless hooks that hide under a set of long rubber band-like legs. Francis jumps around and snatches bass and any other fish hiding in grasses and under lily pads.

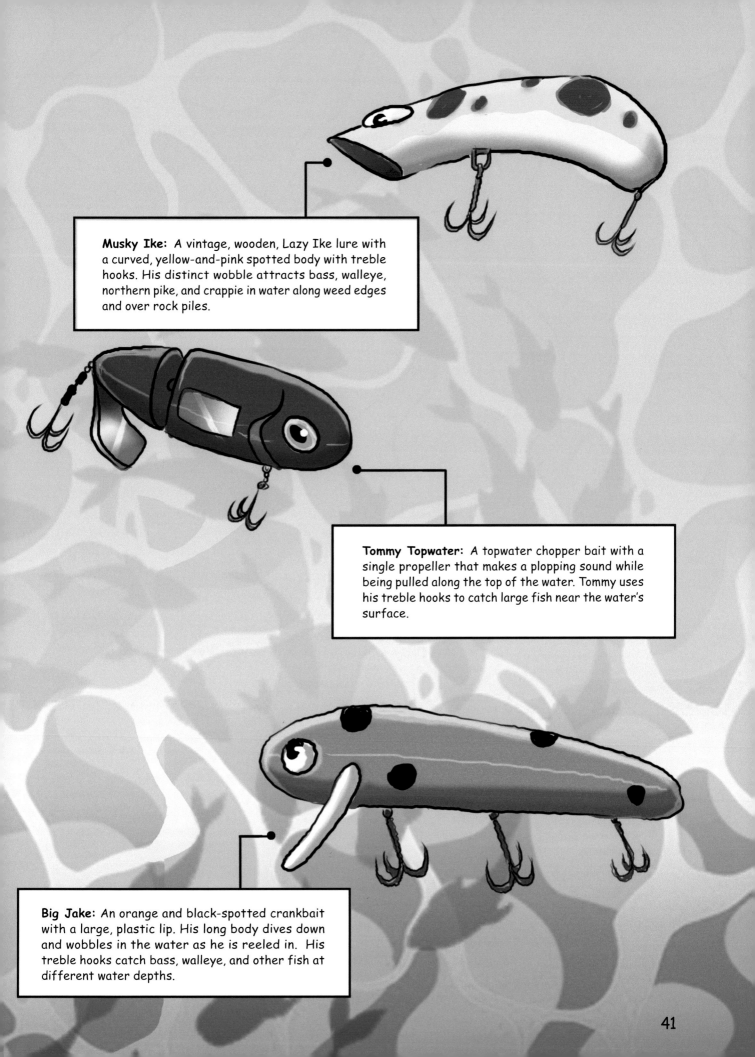

Musky Ike: A vintage, wooden, Lazy Ike lure with a curved, yellow-and-pink spotted body with treble hooks. His distinct wobble attracts bass, walleye, northern pike, and crappie in water along weed edges and over rock piles.

Tommy Topwater: A topwater chopper bait with a single propeller that makes a plopping sound while being pulled along the top of the water. Tommy uses his treble hooks to catch large fish near the water's surface.

Big Jake: An orange and black-spotted crankbait with a large, plastic lip. His long body dives down and wobbles in the water as he is reeled in. His treble hooks catch bass, walleye, and other fish at different water depths.

Printed in the United States
by Baker & Taylor Publisher Services